Who's in Charge?

An exposition of the supremacy of apostolic love

Dr Primitive

All scripture quotations are taken from the New King James Version of the Holy Bible. Copyright©1980 by Thomas Nelson Inc. Used by permission. All rights reserved

Copyright © 2012 Dr. Primitive

All rights reserved. No part of this publication may be reproduced, stored in a retrieval system, or transmitted in any form or by any means, electronic, mechanical, photocopying, recording, or otherwise, without the prior written permission of the publisher.

ISBN: 978-1-60383-420-9

Published by:
Heart Publishing
PO Box 250
Rush City, MN 55069

www.heartofthefather.net

David R. Nichols

Printed in the United States of America and the United Kingdom

Table of Contents

Introduction 5

Chapter One- Can You Believe It? 7

Chapter Two- Are You Out of Your Mind? 25

Chapter Three- The Past Conditions the Future 35

Chapter Four- Jesus: Five-fold in one Man 45

Chapter Five- Who's in Charge in the NT Church? 49

Chapter Six- Who's in Charge in Church History? 55

Chapter Seven- Apostolic Ministry in the Present 67

Chapter Eight- Receiving Apostles in a Celebrity Culture .. 77

Chapter Nine- What Are the Apostles in Charge of? 87

Conclusion 101

Scriptures for Apostolic Love 103

Introduction

This is a book about foundations. It was written from a primitive perspective. By that I mean that the example of Jesus and the apostles is the one to be followed. The primitive version of anything is the earliest, and therefore the most undefiled example. There are many ideas and formats of leadership in the modern and post-modern world. But the cry for authentic NT Christianity is emerging from across the earth. The world that was so loved by the Father that He sent His Son deserves to see and hear the Gospel as it was originally, or primitively, presented. Quite simply, that is with signs, wonders, healings, and manifestations of the real power of God. I have no interest in hype, histrionics, or crowd manipulation. I believe that when Jesus is glorified and the Holy Spirit is allowed to move in power, the love of the Father will become known, and human hearts will turn from dead superstitions to the true and living God. I also have little interest in political correctness, or religious correctness, if you prefer. I want all God has to offer, all the time, and in every situation.

In this book I set forth the case that the ministry of apostles is the key to the restoration of primitive Christianity. The unrestrained ministry of teachers has been in the way of this for a long time. Failing to heed the example of ancient Israel, the church repeated its mistakes and fell into the powerless mode of existence we see in church history. But Jesus is changing all that and He is calling the church of today back to a Kingdom expression of power and love that can only be led by apostles. The underlined words in this book are Greek and Hebrew words from the texts of the Bible in the original languages. I explain and define each of these in the statements that follow their occurrences.

The stories told in this book are all my own experiences. I have tried to relate them just as they happened, without embellishing them at all. You will have to decide whether I am mad, or a proper servant of Jesus Christ. By the time you have finished this book, you will make a decision. Will you believe that the church of Jesus Christ can live and move in the power and love He designed for it? I pray that you will believe it!

Dr Primitive

Chapter One- Can You Believe It?

"You may not be able to continue these meetings; the militants have threatened violence because of this Gospel message!" exclaimed the chief of police. We were in Giddalur, South India. The first night's meeting was wonderful. Many people were healed of diseases by the power that is in the name of Jesus. Hundreds were saved, confessing their sins. Now we were up against strong opposition. The local Hindu militants were determined to shut us down. Even though we had the police permission for the meetings, the chief of police was not about to let his city erupt into violence. I knew that prevailing prayer was the only thing that could help us break through.

There was an unusual level of unity among the Christian leaders in this town. The most visible supporter of the meetings was Father Ilura, the Roman Catholic priest. The Anglican (Church of South India) bishop was in town this week, attending the meetings with joy. There were leading pastors from liturgical, evangelical, and pentecostal persuasions, but they were in unity to see the Gospel advance in power in their town.

When I heard this message from the chief of police, I said to Stephen, our crusade director, "Please find Father Ilura, the bishop, and two of these other pastors! We are going to pray together!" He went and got them, and the six of us began to pray. Our unity was not based on our doctrine, or even in our individual practices of Christianity. Our unity was based in a person, the Lord Jesus Christ, whose presence was becoming real in Giddalur. After we prayed, and the gifts of the Holy Spirit manifested, especially prophecy, we knew what to do. Within one hour, these four local leaders had a meeting with the MLA- member of legislative assembly. This man was the political authority in this region. Each pastor was given five minutes to speak. They presented the case of the meetings, and how they would enhance the life and welfare of the city. After the pastors spoke, the MLA stood up and said, "These militants are not going to complain to the police anymore. If they want to say anything more, they will have to come into this room, and stand before me. And when they do, this is what I will tell them: 'You leave these people alone. They are only doing good in this city. The sick bodies of the people are being healed; the demons are being cast out.'" Then the MLA said, "The meetings will go on. I will call the chief of police and tell him so!" Our four pastors left the meeting with joy. And the meetings did go on, until thousands were saved, with many more being healed and delivered. There was great joy in that city!

A series of events occurred 2000 years ago that changed the history of mankind forever. It began with prophecies uttered and written hundreds of years ahead of time. The earliest of these prophecies was spoken out of the mouth of God Himself. After the first two human beings, Adam and Eve, sinned against God, a prophecy came. In Genesis 3:15 God said, "I will put enmity between you and the woman and between your seed and her Seed; He shall bruise your head, and you shall bruise His heel."

Immediately after the first rebellion against God's way, the prophetic promise pointed to the coming of the Seed of the woman. In other words, the human race would be so involved in the answer to sin that one of its own would crush the head of the serpent. In the centuries that followed, prophecies continued to point to the coming of this One. In Isaiah 7:14 we read, "…Behold, the virgin shall conceive and bear a Son, and shall call His name Immanuel." This Hebrew word means "God with us." But how could a human being be God?

Obviously, there is no shortage of pretenders on the stage of human history. Many men, and even some women, have come, claiming to be God. Greek mythology has gods and goddesses, and some who seem to stand in between, partly god, and partly man. Hercules is one such individual, and Achilles is another. But we never read about these two, or any other like them, having the audacity to forgive sin. The religions of the world have no shortage of beings who are human and who possess god-like characteristics. But again, none of these tell us they can forgive sin, and then proceed to actually do it.

Jesus came into a world filled with stories and beliefs about deliverers, divine men that thrilled the imaginations of the ancient peoples. But Jesus was born into a racial, religious and cultural setting in which the people had learned the hard way that there was only one God. Seventy years of captivity in Babylon had finally convinced the Jews that idol worship of gods and goddesses could not help them. Their decision to obey God's messengers, the prophets, meant forsaking all other gods to serve the One True God alone. The life-world of these people, the Jews, held a tolerance and respect, and sometimes, a desire for miracles. Their Scriptures included many accounts of God interacting with the human world by interventions from the spirit realm. And although most people believed that God did miracles in the past, few, if any, could say that they had seen a genuine miracle of God right before their eyes.

But then, miracles began to happen one after another. The timing for prophecies to be fulfilled came together. A couple named Zacharias and Elizabeth conceived and bore a child at the age of eighty. He would be known as John the Baptist. The angel Gabriel appeared to a young virgin named Mary. And although she was promised in marriage to a man named Joseph, the angel told her she would bear a son who should be named Jesus! All this was to be done by the power of the Holy Spirit. You can read about this in the Gospel of Luke, chapters one and two. "In the fullness of time, God sent forth His Son, born of a woman, born under the law, to redeem those who were under the law, that we might receive the adoption as sons," Paul the apostle wrote in Galatians 4:4, 5. By being born of a woman, the Son of God became a man. He did not cease being God, and yet He was a man. This is the greatest of all miracles, the fulfillment of the prophecies; the revelation of God's saving power from heaven itself, Jesus the Christ.

Many people who believed that God did miracles, but who had never seen one, now began to experience miracles personally. Water turned into wine. Blinded eyes were opened. Deaf ears were unstopped. Lepers were cleansed supernaturally. And then, the unthinkable began to happen. Jesus began to raise dead people back to life. It was the resurrection of Lazarus that caused the most trouble.

The religious leaders of Jesus' day were individuals who took seriously their stewardship of the belief structures of the Jewish people. The Pharisees were learned teachers of the law. Under God, their supreme authority from the past was Moses, the prophet of God. The past can be a comfortable place when God begins to shake the present. So it was with the Pharisees. They could quote lengthy passages of the Law by heart. They knew the prophecies that I mentioned above. But when the fulfillment of those prophecies was standing right in front of them, healing the sick and casting out demons, they could not understand what they were seeing and hearing. The Sadducees had a greater problem with Jesus than the Pharisees. Their belief structure did not include miracles, or the existence of angels or demons. They had no shelf in their intellectual warehouse for a Christ who was constantly casting out demons and healing the sick with miraculous power. So both groups began to oppose Jesus. Think about this. The representatives of God's truth in their generation could not see the Truth embodied in the person of Jesus. The greatest amount of opposition to Jesus did not come from sinners, tax collectors, and prostitutes. It came from the trained, educated, scholars and teachers of the law. ***Those who knew the most, believed the least.***

Jesus promised that His followers would do the same works He did, and even greater works (John 14:12). These works have continued down through the ages of church history. But even today, modern Pharisees (those who believe miracles are possible, but do not expect to see one today) and Sadducees (those who do not believe healings and miracles are possible) are still denying the living power of Jesus in His followers.

Sometimes, God has mercy on us that can only be described as amazing grace. I was conducting a crusade in a village in India when the locals decided to have a separate meeting for the ladies in a particular church. Our pastor's school was occurring at another location in the city. My wife, Sherry and I arrived at the site for the ladies' conference, for she was the main speaker. Hundreds of ladies had gathered at the church, and I dutifully deposited her at the door. I was to be the next speaker at the pastors' school on the other side of town, and I headed for the vehicle. Standing in my path was the pastor of this church, where the ladies were meeting. He said, "Oh, Brother Nichols, you are here! Please come to my house for tea and crumpets." Sometimes seeming interruptions are occasions for incredible ministry. My mind was on the dozens of pastors at our school, but somehow I knew I had to go with this pastor to his house. When we got there, he introduced me to his wife, Agnes, who had a condition of paralysis in her feet for over eight years. As I sat across from them, they gave me all the details. The Holy Spirit was downloading into my spirit, "Pray for this woman, pray for this woman." Suddenly I said to the pastor, "I believe God wants to heal Agnes today!" He looked quite shocked. I stood up and took

Agnes by the hands, and she stood up, but she could not walk. I said to the pastor, "Please help me pray." He gave a muffled answer and just sat there. I turned to praying for Agnes. After a couple of minutes of saying all the right things, there was a measure of the presence of God there, but we were not breaking through, and I knew it. I stopped praying and looked down at the pastor and said, "Man, this is your wife, please help me pray for her, God wants to heal her." Once again, he gave a muffled response and just sat there. I pressed in to pray for Agnes again. Soon she fell back into the couch she had been sitting on. The power of God was all over her. I believed she was healed! I excused myself and went out the front door of the house. I was sitting on a chair, putting my shoes back on when I looked over my right shoulder. Here came Agnes, walking out of the house on her feet, *healed by the name of Jesus!!* Some girls came from somewhere and guided her into the back of the church housing the ladies' meeting. The crowd was exuberant to see her walking. For about half of the ladies, this was their pastor's wife.

After the pastors' school was over that day, I was standing, talking with some of the members of our Indian team and some local people. I told of the healing of Agnes that morning at the pastor's house. The local people were quiet. I asked if something was wrong. They said, "Sir, you must understand; that is a cessationist church." This kind of church is one where they believe that Jesus and the apostles in Acts did miracles and healings, but that there are no miracles today, because they have ceased, thus the name, cessationist. When I heard this I said, "Oops!" Now please bear in mind that I went into the situation innocent. I did not know they were that kind of church. I wasn't trying to prove anything, except that Jesus is the healer, and He wanted to relieve the suffering of Agnes by healing her. But in the hours that followed, I began to get down on myself. "You should have checked first." "They don't believe in healing, and now the pastor's wife is healed." These and many other thoughts ran through my mind.

That night, the pastor himself came up and invited myself and the whole team to come to their house for a meal. As we arrived there the next day, I thought, "Now I'm going to get it." Things were pleasant through the whole meal, and then the pastor stood next to me and put his hand on my shoulder. With his other hand he motioned for me to come into a back room of the house. As the two of us stood in the room, he began pulling out x-rays and medical records of himself. After telling me everything that was wrong with him, he said, "Would you pray for me, too?" Now think about this for a moment. This man was seventy years old. As far as I know, he had been taught in seminary that even though Jesus and the apostles of the NT healed and did miracles, there is no healing today. As far as I know, he taught this himself through his entire ministry. And here he is now, asking to be prayed for to be healed! I said, "Yes, I'll pray for you." And I did. The next morning, I stepped out of the hotel onto the street of the city. There was the pastor, with a group of people. I walked up to him and said, "How are you today?" He said, "My body is very happy!" I rejoiced, but I said, "What does this mean? Are you healed?" He could not say the word "healed" but continued rejoicing in his healing. His body is very happy! The extravagant grace and mercy of God overflowed, and healed a man who didn't even believe in healing in today's world! What a God! And what a way to establish the truth of Jesus' healing power in today's world!

There must be a difference between the knowledge that comes from the gathering of information, and that which comes by revelation. The Pharisees and Sadducees had the best information anyone could have in their day. If you asked them, they would tell you they were in touch with revelation, as well. But when the revelation of the fullness of God stood in front of them with skin on, they called Him Beelzebub (Matthew 12:24). This Beelzebub was actually a Philistine deity, a ruling evil spirit that was well known in Jesus' day. The Pharisees had turned in upon themselves so much, that their knowledge, rooted in information without revelation, required their opposition to the One who created Moses!

How can this be? How can people who are trained in the Scriptures, some of whom are even anointed by God to perform their ministry, deny the revelation of the Son of God? There is a kind of zeal in the teaching gift when it is not submitted to apostolic and prophetic authority that is destructive. This zeal combines itself with pride in knowledge to oppose what cannot be controlled. And Jesus could not be controlled by the religious hypocrisy of the Pharisees and Sadducees. Neither could the apostles in the book of Acts. Nor could hundreds of simple Christian believers whose names we do not know. Through the ages of church history they just kept healing the sick and casting out demons, even though these practices brought them into persecution by church leaders and even to their deaths in some cases.

If you were to pick up the four gospels, Matthew, Mark, Luke, and John, and read them; then if the book of Acts fell open in your hands, you would certainly be impressed by the power of God. You would have read of the coming of Jesus, the Son of God into the world. You would now know how He healed people and did miracles. Your understanding of the Kingdom of Heaven would be profound, because Jesus advanced the Kingdom wherever He went. By word and deed, the advance of the Kingdom could not be stopped by demons, principalities, human governments, or any other force. In Acts chapter one, Jesus handed off the task of advancing the Kingdom to His followers. And advance it they did. Starting from Jerusalem to Judea, and on to Samaria, the Gospel of the Kingdom went to the ends of the earth. It seemed as if clusters of Christians existed everywhere. These Christians were doing the same things Jesus did, healing the sick and casting out demons. In the hostile environment of the ancient Roman Empire, Christianity spread like wildfire. Amazingly, these Christians were not only willing to live for Jesus; they were willing to die for Him. And die they did, hunted down and persecuted, caught by their enemies. They were beaten, imprisoned, and tortured, but they would not recant. They had an example in front of them always, their Leader, the Lord Jesus Christ. Arrested, imprisoned, beaten, and in possession of the power to free Himself, Jesus went to the Cross. When Jesus died on the cross, it wasn't a religious object at all. It was an instrument of extreme torture used by the Roman government to keep subject peoples under their tyranny. No one in his right mind would desire a cross before Jesus died on His. But Jesus went on before, preparing a Way that many would follow. And follow they did, spreading Christianity, not as a religion, but as a way of life, death, and resurrection. By the end of the book of Acts the world was turned upside down (Acts 17:6).

Compare these outcomes with the efforts of Western Christianity in our times. In the last two centuries, more man-hours and money have been spent on Christian causes than the early Christians could have dreamed. And the outcomes have been so far behind what they accomplished that we seem to be only dreaming when we think that in our times cities could be shaken by the power of God; that nations could repent and turn to Jesus. Why is this? What happened that changed the simplicity, power, and purity of the message of Jesus into religious form, ritual, and powerless external piety? Certainly we could talk about the engagement of Christianity with differing cultural and ideological forces around the globe for many centuries, but we would only tire ourselves in the process, for this has been done many times. The problem is an old one. The Christians were not the first to face it, although sadly, over time they repeated the mistake of ancient Israel before them. What is this mistake, you ask? It is allowing the teachers to rule, and especially when they rule in the absence of kingly authority. Why is this so? Because teachers are wired to minister to the mind. Ministry to the mind is valid and important. Our minds were created by God to be used by us for His glory. But the track record of human minds submitting to God by the teaching gift alone is not good. Check through the Old Testament, then move on to the New, and you will find that more often than not, God is overruling the mind of man. Continue on through church history, and you will find centuries full of examples of the mind of man creating more problems than it solves. In this book we will explore the failures of Israel, and then of the Church, to attempt to understand God's way of righteousness, peace and joy in the Holy Spirit. The message and impact of Christianity is not in the first place a reasoned, logical system of thought. It is based on the most improbable, illogical collection of ideas that has ever been brought together. Once the founder was placed on a cross, and that placement of Him there was put in the center of the movement, all intellectual bets were off.

Our meetings in Giddalur were very powerful in the Holy Spirit, but I will never forget the last night. As the meeting was winding down, Father Ilura came up on the stage. He said, "I'm sorry I couldn't be here last night. I had a disturbance out in a village that needed my attention." I said, "Oh, that's fine sir, we didn't expect you to be here when you were needed there." He said, "Five teachers in my school in the village rose up in rebellion and locked out the priests and nuns." Then he said, "Those five are here tonight; they heard the message, and they want to pray with you!" This apostolic leader had been such a blessing to us through the week we were in Giddalur. He had blessed us many times in many ways. Now it was time to bless him in return.

I said to Father Ilura, "Bring the five teachers up here. I will speak with them." As he began moving to get the five men, he turned his head toward me and said, "They need to be converted!" As the teachers stood in front of me, I gave them Jesus in about five minutes. I asked if they were ready to confess their sins. We held hands in a circle and all five of them repeated the sinner's prayer. Then I stepped forward and held each of them in my arms for about 5-6 minutes, letting the perfect love of the Father flow through me into them. They wept like babies! It was a moment of heaven on earth! When we were finished, I said, "You men are all teachers in Father Ilura's school, is this correct?" They said yes. I said, "You teachers are the ones who have the homework. I want you to go to Father Ilura, and ask him to forgive you." Like a line of puppies, they went down off the platform to find Father Ilura.

Meanwhile, as I was ministering to the teachers on the platform, Father Ilura went down and stood on the ground in front of the platform. Three of our team members finished their praying for the sick, and were walking together when they encountered Father Ilura. He stopped them and exclaimed, "This power that is on you people, what is it?" They said, "Sir, it is the baptism in the Holy Spirit!" Father Ilura said, "I want this. How do I get this?" They said, "We will lay our hands on you, the power of God will come over you, and you will be soaked in the Holy Spirit." Father Ilura said no more, and extended his hands into the air. The team laid their hands on him, and he was baptized in the Holy Spirit, speaking in a language he never learned! I believe this is the ministry of Jesus in this present age, the power of the Holy Spirit, not the power of human intellect. There is no way either Father Ilura or I could have solved his problem with our human intellectual abilities. But when we yielded to the Spirit of Jesus, and manifested the love of the Father, the Kingdom came in power! The five teachers were reconciled to Father Ilura's apostolic leadership, and they now function in unity!

May I remind you that in I Corinthians 1:22, 23 Paul the apostle states that the cross is a <u>skandalon</u> to the Jews, and <u>moria</u> to the Gentiles? A <u>skandalon</u> is a stumbling block, an offense to the sensibilities of normal people. <u>Moria</u> is foolishness. Our English word moron comes from this family of Greek words. It must be a part of the genius of God to create a being, man, with an intellectual mind and reasoning powers, and then require the sacrifice of these in order to know Him. In the ancient world, no one associated a cross with any kind of salvation. In the Roman world, crosses were places where extreme criminals were executed. It would be like saying in our present world that the way we know God is by the electric chair. We could bring our hymns into the modern world and sing, "At the electric chair, at the electric chair, where I first saw the light, and the burdens of my heart rolled away!" And as if this were not enough for our minds, if you can accept this offense, you also have to believe that the cross was exactly what God had in mind, and on the third day Jesus was raised from the dead! No wonder the Romans thought they were crazy!

Chapter Two- Are You Out of Your Mind?

Have you ever wondered why we as human beings sometimes feel conflicted inside? Many times we know what is right to do, but then we do the opposite. Our Western culture teaches us to live from our minds, because, after all, we wouldn't want to be considered an emotional person. In the practice of living from our minds, we foster an inner belief that logic, reason, and rationality will lead us to the truth. The strain upon our mental faculties is enormous as we labor to process huge amounts of data in order to come to the correct conclusion.

Part of the problem is that our minds operate by thoughts, and our minds are constantly in a battle. While you may think that you are in control of your mind and thoughts, you actually have thoughts every day that are not your thoughts. This is because you are a spirit being living in a universe inhabited by other spirit beings. Spirit beings produce thoughts. God Himself is a spirit being (John 4:24) who has always been, and always will be. He is constantly thinking thoughts. In Jeremiah 29:11 He says, "I know the thoughts I think toward you, says the Lord, thoughts of good and not of harm, to give you a future and a hope." In Psalm 139:17, 18 He says, "How precious also are your thoughts to me, O God! How great is the sum of them! If I should count them, they would be more in number than the sand." As the ultimate spirit being, God does incredible amounts of thinking, past, present, and future.

There is another source of thoughts, and that is the human mind. Humans were created in the image of God (Genesis 1:27). Our ability to produce thoughts is based on the fact that we are in God's image. Dogs are wonderful animals most of the time, but they are not in God's image, and they do not produce thoughts. They may have reflexes, responses, and vocalizations that carry meaning, but they do not have thoughts as humans do. In the physical creation, humans stand unique in the ability to produce thought.

If we could stop here, it would be wonderful, for the only thoughts we would need to be concerned with would be our own and God's. But there is a third group of spirit beings in our universe, and they are also constantly producing thoughts. This is the realm of darkness; Satan, his fallen angels and demon spirits. The thoughts produced by these beings are always destructive. They desire to tear down what God is building up. They desire to contradict the truth of God at every turn. And because God created the mind to operate in freedom, we have a battle on our hands. Which thoughts will we heed? Which thoughts will receive our allegiance and obedience? It is when we believe we are autonomous and can direct our own path that we are set up for deception. If you are convinced you are the only being producing thoughts, while two other realms are constantly trying to influence you by thoughts that are actually in your mind, you will be deceived.

It is important to consider the relationship between the five-fold ministry and the thoughts of the mind. Among these five from Ephesians 4:11, the apostle and prophet speak for God from heaven, while the evangelist, pastor, and teacher speak for God from earth. When these five are in proper relationship with one another, they balance and complement one another. When the apostle and prophet are isolated to themselves, all the speaking for God is from heaven, and it may or may not have relevance to the people of earth. When the evangelist, pastor, or teacher is isolated to himself, with no prophetic or apostolic correction, the speech will tend in a humanistic direction. This is most dangerous for teachers, because they are entrusted with the processing of data which should lead to the expression of the truth. Have you ever wondered how teachers from different denominations can teach "truths" which are so diametrically opposed to one another? They all use the same Scriptures, they supposedly all partake of the same Holy Spirit. They are all speaking from earth for the same Jesus. So the will of man is free. Not so, says the other, "It is bound." "Demons and angels are active in the lives of humans," says one. "There is no relevance of angels or demons to human life, or perhaps they do not exist" says another. "The earth was created in six days," says one. "The earth has been evolving over millions of years," says the other. What is needed in all of this is apostolic and prophetic correction.

When we turn to the subject of revival, spiritual life, and the move of God, we enter a battleground. Often, these times of refreshing are accompanied by phenomena that seem new. Sometimes there are manifestations of actions and reactions that "should not happen in church." People jump up and down; they speak in languages they never learned. They run in the aisles, they fall down as they are being prayed for. How do we decide which of these are valid? Who will we trust?

Teachers will decide from the mind, making rational decisions, speaking from the earth. Prophets will speak from heaven, and will excite the emotions. It is the responsibility of the apostles to require a meeting in the heart, where the mind and emotions meet. This is where love can take a seat of honor above knowledge. Love can find a way which is foreign to the mind and yet pleasing to the emotions without giving in to their excesses. Love is the apostolic mandate. Love is greater than faith. Love is greater than hope. The greatest of these (gifts and fruit of the spirit) is love (I Corinthians 13:13).

But within the community of faith there have always been teachers. They are one of God's greatest gifts. They are charged with the responsibility of transmitting the knowledge about God to the masses. In the Old Testament, there was always the reproach of serving a God who was miraculous. Most of the time, when you encounter this God, He is out of the box, doing something revelatory that is drawing His people to Him by their hearts. Being delivered from their enemies by one man with the jawbone of a donkey, or a lad killing the giant with a stone and a sling, or by 300 men armed with pitchers, clay pots, and trumpets defeating 135,000 trained soldiers who had spears, shields, and chariots. It's as if there is a division here between the knowledge *about* God and the direct knowledge *of God*. Teachers spend most of their time studying and transmitting knowledge about God. This is a knowledge which comes through reading, being taught themselves, studying, and other rational processes. The teachers may describe revelations, miracles, signs and wonders, but these are no more than that, descriptions alone, unless there is demonstration. There is another kind of knowledge, that which comes from revelation, instantly, and immediately given into the heart of a person. This is the realm of prophets and prophetic revelation. It is uncomfortable for many within the community of faith because it so often bypasses the rational thought processes of logic and reflection. But this is how God has chosen to make Himself known so many times in Scripture, by prophetic revelation. This is the knowledge *of God*, and it is designed by Him to go hand-in-hand with the knowledge *about God*.

I experienced the difference between these two kinds of knowledge on a field in India. In 2006, we were conducting a seven-night crusade in the city of Nandikotkur. By the sixth night, we had already seen thousands come to Jesus as savior. Many people had been healed and received miracles. There were about 33,000 people present there that night. As I sat on my chair on the platform, I was in a euphoric mood of thankfulness to God for allowing me to see, and actually lead, such a move of God upon a city and region. The worship team was doing very well, the Presence of the living God was coming stronger, and I was rejoicing. Suddenly, in the middle of all this reverie, *it began to rain!* In an outdoor crusade meeting, this is about the worst thing that can happen. If it rains very long, the crowd will begin to melt away like sugar. I looked up at an angle into the sky, and saw the moon in clear view. I couldn't see the sky directly above, because the lights were too bright. I don't know if there were clouds there or not. I just knew it was raining and I was about to lose my crowd before I preached. As I looked down to the ground, I saw my Indian leadership team in a huddle. These men of God were discussing urgently what we should do. In a moment, our main leader came running up on the platform, knelt in front of me and said, "Here's what we think we should do; I'll stop the worship team and then introduce you. You can preach a quick message, give a quick altar call, and perhaps we can salvage some results from the rain." I looked at him intently and said, "Make it so!" And he did. So far, we were operating in our minds, making rational decisions based on observation of the data. On my journey from the back of the platform to the front, God broke in. The Holy Spirit said to me, "No, we're not doing the quick thing." I heard Him in my spirit very clearly. But by now I was standing in front of 33,000 people with a mike in my hand, and I didn't know what to say. My few moments of quick preparation in light of the rain had been overruled by the Spirit of God. I decided to take a risk. I only had one piece of revelation, and I acted on it. "We're not doing the quick thing." I opened my mouth and began to speak. As I did, I listened to myself to see what I was saying because I was not rationally processing what was coming out of my mouth. It was like speaking in tongues, except it was in English, being translated into Telegu by our faithful interpreter. I said, "You people are looking at me, because you believe if I pray a prayer, God will stop this rain. But I say to you that the One True God is waiting to hear your prayer. If you will pray to Him, He will stop this rain, and we'll go on with this meeting!" I took a step back, and a thought came to my mind. It said, "Nichols, you are an idiot! 25,000 of these people are Hindus and Muslims and you just told them that God would answer their prayer!" I said, "Get behind me, Satan!" And I began praying my own prayer into the mike. The voices of 8,000 Christians and 25,000 Hindus and Muslims united in prayer. The sound grew louder and louder until it reached a crescendo. Then something cracked in the air, *and it stopped raining!!* Suddenly, everyone was rejoicing, and it was really easy to preach that night after the rain stopped. I just had to say, "Remember the God who stopped the rain a few minutes ago?" Everyone would nod their heads. The revelatory knowledge of God is always accompanied by the supernatural power of God. God never told us to figure out the best strategies for doing His work. He told us to trust Him, listen to Him, and obey. The rest would be up to Him, and He does not fail! That night I had a clear lesson in the difference between *information* and *revelation*, the difference between *knowledge about God* and *knowledge of/from God*. The difference in outcomes was great! If we had persevered in our knowledge about God, a few dozen people would likely have been saved after being soaked in rain. But instead, 3600 people stepped forward to receive Jesus, and they were all dry, because the rain had been stopped by God!

There is a proper place for the knowledge about God. We need clear teaching of the content, meaning, and correct interpretation of Scripture. It is the bedrock and foundation of our faith. The problem is that the dispensers of the knowledge *about* God and the dispensers of the knowledge *of* God have a hard time trusting each other. This is because they are coming from two different orientations. They need a power of cohesion greater than themselves to hold them together. God Himself has provided such a power. In the OT, it is the authority of God represented in the king. In the NT, it is the authority of God represented in the apostle. This kingly, governing authority has the ability to draw the best from the teachers and from the prophets and present it to the people. When the teachers rule instead of the apostles, the power of God is exchanged for information, the reproach of the cross and resurrection are exchanged for eloquent expositions, and Christianity is widely perceived as powerless.

Chapter Three- The Past Conditions the Future

There are many lessons we can learn from the story of Israel in the OT. They had a unique relationship with God among the nations. The living God revealed Himself to Israel in many striking ways. The prophets were the spokesmen and women for God to Israel. They heard the voice of God and prophesied based on what they saw and heard. There was a commonly held understanding that a few individuals had the ability to hear God directly. So throughout the OT, we find kings and other leaders coming to the prophets to receive the word of the Lord. The first mention of a prophet is in Genesis 20:7, where Abraham is called a prophet. The setting is that Abraham told Abimelech that Sarah was his sister. Abimelech took her to his place, but did not touch her. Nevertheless, the wrath of God began to come to Abimilech's household because of Sarah. He was instructed by God to have Abraham pray for him, *because Abraham was a prophet.* The strong implication was that God would hear his prayer and release the household from their infirmities. And this is exactly what happened.

This special relationship with God gives the prophets a special status in the OT. They were viewed as a special class of people who were to devote their time to seeking God. Many of the kings of the OT had court prophets, whose responsibility it was to advise the king from heaven and the voice of God. The OT prophets had access to heaven for the welfare and peace of the nation. Many times they were called upon by God to confront rulers with their sin. A most famous case of this was the sin of King David with Bathsheba. The story is found in II Samuel 11 and 12. After David had committed adultery with Bathsheba, he had her husband, Uriah, sent to the front lines of the battle. Then, under the command from David, the troops pulled back from Uriah and left him to fight alone. He was killed by the enemy soldiers, but really, he was killed by David and his command. David thought he had done a good job of covering up his sin. He took Bathsheba as his wife and she bore him a child. But then Nathan the prophet showed up at David's house. The living God had shown him exactly what had taken place, and Nathan communicated the Word of the Lord by means of a parable. A man had an ewe lamb that was like a daughter to him. It drank from his cup and was held in his bosom. A rich neighbor of his had a visitor, and instead of preparing one of his own sheep, he took the lamb of the poor man, and prepared it for his guest. Upon hearing this, David was enraged and declared that the rich man should die. Nathan leaned forward and said, "You are the man!" You see, the parable was really about David, Uriah, and Bathsheba. Then Nathan proceeded to pronounce the judgment of God upon David and his household for this sin.

The status and role of the prophet in ancient Israel was indeed a powerful one. They did not hesitate to bring the word of the Lord as they were shown by God. They were used by God to bring victories of amazing proportions, and judgments which were equally amazing. In the leadership structure of Israel, it was their responsibility to hear God's voice accurately and clearly. Kings either listened or disobeyed, but always, the word of the Lord prevailed. Priests became corrupt at times. Then God would raise up a Samuel to rebuke them, and straighten the course of the nation.

The kings were the last office of the three to be established in Israel. They also carried the most authority in the human realm. They had the power of their armies and power of life and death over the individual. The kings of Israel are to be compared to the apostles in the NT. When they were righteous, the kings did much good in bringing peace and tranquility to the nation. The source of the power was an authority from heaven to command the people. David is usually acknowledged as the greatest king of Israel. Through his powerful leadership, the enemies were defeated. True worship was restored. The presence of God was revered in a way it was not before. This is the true exercise of the kingly/apostolic authority. When the kings allowed their mandate from heaven to be polluted by the corruption of the agenda of earth, they failed. When they allowed their mandate from heaven to be augmented by the ministries of the prophets and priests, they had success and they prospered.

One of the greatest illustrations of the negative in these relationships is the story of Ahab told in I Kings 22. Here we have a king who consistently sold himself to do evil. He surrounded himself with a collection of court prophets, who told him what he wanted to hear. But on the eve of the greatest battle of his life, he reluctantly calls for Micaiah. This prophet of God is warned to fall in with the "party line" and affirm the king's plans. But instead he recounts his vision of all Israel being scattered, and having no shepherd. This means that Ahab will die if he goes into this planned battle with the enemy. Ahab says, "Feed this fellow on bread and water until I return in peace." Micaiah says, "If you return at all, God has not spoken by me!" And as you know, Ahab died after being hit by an "errant arrow." Prophets had the ultimate responsibility for speaking from heaven. Even kings had to listen and obey. From the time of Moses and Aaron onward, the priests also functioned as the teachers of the Law. The common people were to receive the righteousness of God imparted by teaching through the priests. The prophets and kings were there to balance the ministry to the whole person. When these three were in harmony with each other, Israel prospered. When they were at odds with each other, there was chaos, and sometimes even calamity.

The priests were also special representatives of God to the people. Their ministry was that of offering the sacrifices to God for the sins of the people. The first mention of a priest is Melchizedek in Genesis 14:18. He was king of Salem and priest of God most high. Melchizedek received tithes from Abraham when he returned from defeating the kings. For this reason, the author of Hebrews states that Melchizedek was greater than Abraham (Hebrews 7:5-7). Since Abraham is the father of Levi, the Levitical order of priesthood is inferior to the Melchizedek order. It seems that through centuries of OT history, the Melchizedek priesthood was an unfulfilled promise while the Levitical priesthood conducted the daily and annual sacrifices in the tabernacle and later in the temple. But when Jesus came, as Hebrews chapter 7 makes clear, he fulfilled the Melchizedek priesthood. He is even now acting as High Priest in heaven itself.

One of the saddest parts of the story of Israel in the OT is that over time, they could not sustain first the unity and then even the existence of these three offices. The first of the three offices to cease was that of the kings. Through the prophets, God had warned Israel many times that their sin would lead them to judgment. For the sake of David, Israel's greatest king, generation after generation, God suspended and postponed judgment. But finally a day of reckoning came. Nebuchadnezzar, king of Babylon, came to Jerusalem with his armies three times: 605BC, 597BC, and 587/6BC. During this last visit, he and his soldiers destroyed the city walls and the temple itself. He also ended the physical Davidic kingly order, when the Israelite king Zedekiah was taken captive. All this is recorded in II Chronicles 36. When Zedekiah was deposed, the end of an era was manifested. From then onwards in Israel's history, the office of king was abolished. The political leadership of the nation was given over to governors appointed by foreign kings. One of the strands of the three-fold cord was now severed. The spiritual leadership of the nation was now split between the prophets and the priests. After the seventy year captivity in Babylon, the temple was rebuilt, and the priestly order began again to do its ministry of sacrificing for the sins of the people. The prophets had been there all along, with such notable individuals as first Ezekiel and Daniel, and later, Zechariah and Haggai, leading the way to knowing God.

The rebuilding of the Temple was accomplished without the presence of an Israelite king. Ezra, a scribe trained in the Law, led the way back to a passionate observance of the decrees of Moses. It became clear that God was really passionate about idolatry, to the point that He caused His own nation, Israel, to be taken captive because of it. So Ezra was certainly doing the right thing in teaching against idolatry. The prophets of that era also denounced idolatry over and over. But the prophets did not fixate on idolatry. They thundered out against every kind of evil that was against the nature of God. They addressed the surrounding nations for their sins, as well. As inspired oracles of God, they balanced the teaching priests. The two-fold cord of prophets and teachers functioned together for about two hundred years. Then came the end of the era of the inspired prophets. When Malachi, the last prophet of the OT order, died in about 350BC, the living voice of inspired prophecy was silenced. Now only one strand of the threefold cord was left. What would happen? Since the priests were in charge, the institution of the Temple became the central focus of life in Israel. Alongside the teaching priests, another group was rising in favor and influence with the people. They were called the Pharisees. They were teachers without an office, and they learned to flow between the priests and the political rulers of the day.

A rigid orthodoxy began to emerge. If the heart of God was opposed to idolatry, then this must be the key to knowing God. And as long as we are opposing idolatry, we must be pleasing to God, right? In the absence of kingly (apostolic) and prophetic correction, the teachers began to rely more and more on the past. Very few, if any miracles were happening in the present, but the past was full of miracles, especially the time of Moses and Aaron. Everyone knew that miracles are an important indicator of the presence and favor of God. So the Pharisees became ardent followers of Moses, the lawgiver. This gave the Pharisees contact with the miracles they believed in with their heads. These miracles were comfortable, because they happened hundreds of years ago. They were comfortable because they surrounded the ministry of Moses, universally acknowledged to be the prophet of God. Miracles in the present are not as comfortable, because they force you to make a decision.

We were doing a crusade in a village in Tanzania. I've learned that it is very important to demonstrate healing and miracles to the crowd before I preach. Why should they believe some white man standing on a platform talking loud through a PA system? They should believe us if we do the same things Jesus did. If we do that first, they will listen when we tell them important truths about their lives and their souls. This is especially true in areas where witchcraft and animism have been the main forms of spirituality. I had a word of knowledge for healing of paralysis in the ankles and feet. So I proclaimed that, among other things in a healing expression over the people. A man paralyzed in his feet had been brought to the meeting from 70 kilometers away. He had heard about the festival over the radio. His friends set him down under a tree and left. He sat there all day, waiting for the meeting to start. When the meeting started and the healing proclamation came, the power of God came over him, and he stood up, and began to walk. A few minutes later, he was on our platform, testifying of his healing! We have videotape of this former paralytic dancing with me on the platform in front of the people. The people saw a healing miracle right before their eyes, and they had to make a decision. Who did this? I told them it was Jesus! At the altar call an hour later, hundreds came forward to repent of their sins and start a new life with Jesus! They didn't come because of the brilliant intellectual oratory. I know, I was the preacher. They came because the sight and hearing of an undeniable miracle called them to a decision. Surrounded by the living presence of the living God, they were drawn by His love to be His children. Thank you, Jesus!

So the Pharisees were men of the Law. It is true that God can be known by His laws, but sometimes the God of the laws is left behind. The zeal and teaching of the Pharisees actually helped sustain Israel through times of great strife and tribulation. Through the pressured times of the Maccabees, the mandate against idolatry was tested over and over again. And even the profaning of the temple itself by the Seleucid king Antiochus Epiphanes could not undermine this very valuable lesson. Israel had learned well from the Babylonian captivity. So as we draw nearer and nearer to the time of Christ, we see several tenets firmly embedded in the consciousness of the people, taught by the Pharisees. First, they will die before accepting idolatry. Second, the Law of Moses, as taught by the scribes and Pharisees, is the greatest spiritual value. Third, miracles of the past are to be celebrated, and those of the present are to be suspected. Fourth, a great expectation emerged for a coming deliverer who would restore the prophetic and kingly functions to Israel. The priests were willing to let the Pharisees have their way with the people, so long as they could depend on their support in political struggles. And a huge political struggle was coming: the question of what to do about Jesus of Nazareth.

Chapter Four- Jesus: Five-fold in one Man

The appearance of Jesus here on earth marked the beginning of a whole new epoch in God's dealings with humans. Jesus was God and man at the same time. Jesus was also full of power, compassion, wisdom, and knowledge. In contrast to the failure of Israel in the flesh, Jesus was the embodiment of the fullness of God and man. Into the vacuum created by the end of Israelite kings, Jesus proclaimed, "The Kingdom of Heaven is at hand!" The King of kings had no earthly throne, but the kingly authority of His office was clearly upon Him. Did the Israel of old have 12 tribes? Now it had 12 apostles! And the greatest apostle was Jesus Himself. He was constantly demonstrating that God-given authority in establishing the Kingdom. For over three years, the 12 apostles-in-training watched, were trained, and healed the sick themselves. They had the greatest example of all right in front of them. Jesus is the apostle and high priest of our confession (Hebrews 3:1).

Prophets were involved with the coming of Jesus for hundreds of years before He was born. Isaiah, Micah, Jeremiah, Daniel, and others prophesied the coming of the messiah. He was to be a deliverer and prophet in His own right. And indeed Jesus' words were so prophetic that some thought He was an appearance of one of the prophets of old. But Jesus' task was much greater. He came to restore the prophetic office to its former greatness and beyond. Standing as the prophet like Moses, He superseded Moses by preparing the people of God to be a prophesying people. Moses wished that all God's people were prophets, and that He would put His Spirit upon them all (Numbers 11:25). Jesus fulfilled His promise and poured out the Spirit. Then under the leadership of His apostle Peter, the sons and daughters, young and old, high and low, began to prophesy (Acts 2:16-18). The greatest prophet to ever speak, Jesus, restored the office of the prophet with signs greater than those of Moses, Elijah, or anyone else.

Jesus understood that a five-fold ministry would be necessary to fulfill the three-fold ministry of the Old Testament. His own status as apostle and prophet are clear, but He also functioned at the highest levels of the office of evangelist. Who but Jesus could understand the true condition of the lost? Who was constantly reaching over barriers to extend the Father's love to sinners? Jesus practiced evangelism wherever He went. But even more important, He established an office and ministry of evangelist that would increase and expand the church all over the world. Therefore, when He gave the Great Commission, He was expressing what He Himself had already been doing. This is reaching those who do not know the life-changing message of Jesus, His Cross, and His Resurrection.

More was needed. Jeremiah prophesied that the shepherds would be raised up to feed the people (Jeremiah 23:4). Jesus fulfilled this Scripture and became the Great Shepherd of the sheep (John 10:14). The pastoral care of the people was one of Jesus' greatest concerns in His earthly ministry. He comforted, spoke life, and ministered into the lives of countless persons in Galilee and Judea. An office of ministry came into being: that of pastor.

The ministry of the teacher is never seen more clearly than when we look at Jesus. He taught the truth, no matter what it cost. He confronted the hypocrites and false teachers of His day, never in malice, but always in power and love. When it is uncorrupted by human philosophies, the office and ministry of teacher is a powerful one indeed. Jesus showed us that He was the Teacher of Israel. He left it for the apostle Paul to be the teacher of the Gentiles (I Timothy 2:7). Remember that by the time we come to the life of Jesus, the only office left from the Old Testament was the teaching priests. Jesus elevated the office and ministry of teacher to the highest possible place. He put before us the example of how this mighty gift should work.

The net outcome of the unity of these gifts in Jesus is a ministry that is balanced, not by humanistic demands, but by the need to speak from heaven to earth. Five ministries are needed in order for this to be done at the level Jesus showed us. So Jesus led by demonstrating the Kingdom in power. His teachings and His deeds were accomplished in unity with each other. This is the absolute integrity of Jesus' life. But Jesus also commissioned and sent out an apostolic church that had the power to reproduce itself with changed lives.

Chapter Five- Who's in Charge in the NT Church?

Looking at the power and authority of Jesus' ministry, you would think that a standard was set that would last forever, and it was! Observing the five-fold ministry in the book of Acts, and the rest of the New Testament, you would think the world could be turned upside down, and it was! With a start like this, how could the people of God ever go back to the way it was in the period between the OT and NT? To answer this question, we must examine several scriptures in the New Testament. In Ephesians 2:20 the apostle Paul states that apostles and prophets are the foundation of the church. Teachers, however important they may be, are not the foundation of the NT church. The reason the church in the book of Acts quickly spread everywhere is that it was founded on the statements and actions of the apostles and prophets. By the time the book of Ephesians was written, Paul was merely reporting what had been happening for several decades. Blind eyes were seeing, lame limbs were working again, the dead were being raised. You would almost think Jesus was walking the earth again. Actually, He was, He was present in His apostles, prophets, evangelists, pastors and teachers. With apostles and prophets occupying the foundational roles, the evangelists, pastors, and teachers could each add their own vital and life-giving ministry to the mix. In I Corinthians 12:28 the apostle Paul declares an order in the ministry giftings: first apostles, second prophets, third teachers. When this order is maintained, we can expect to experience the advance of the Kingdom as presented in the NT. When this order is changed, we will see something else. When teachers attempt to be the foundation, and when they move from number three to number one, the foundational values change. The church should have learned this crucial lesson from Israel, but by the second and third centuries AD, the church was well on its way to being a teacher-based operation.

To understand this better, we need to explain the basic differences between apostles and teachers. The differences are in the orientations of the ministries. When apostles are in charge: churches are planted, the sick are healed, the dead are raised, the lost are saved, and the demonized are delivered. All these operations are motivated by love. When teachers are in charge: doctrines are debated, terms are defined, opponents are refuted, and the Gospel is an idea. All these operations are motivated by the desire for more knowledge. It is not that teachers have no love, many of them do. It is that their first and primary instinct is the quest for more knowledge. The rational pursuit of knowledge will inevitably involve the pursuer in the tree of knowledge of good and evil, not the tree of life. And we all know what that decision cost the human race when it was made by our first parents, Adam and Eve (Genesis 2:9, 15-17; 3:1-7).

This should help us understand how it could be that the Pharisees and the chief priests, teachers all, were the most ardent opponents of Jesus Himself. They had the OT memorized. They venerated Moses and the prophets of the past. They were students of the great miracles in Israel's past. But when Jesus began speaking from the tree of life, they couldn't stand it. He violated their traditions. He stepped on their religious pride in knowledge. They couldn't help themselves from speaking from the tree of the knowledge of good and evil. It is this mixture in this tree that is so deadly. Some of its contents are good and some are evil. But out of the tree of life comes love, pure and unadulterated. The Pharisees and chief priests could not stand this comparison, so Jesus had to die. They had no apostolic or prophetic correction above them. There was only the secular authority of Rome represented by Pilate, and they had learned well how to manipulate him.

In light of this, there is another verse we should consider. In I Corinthians 8:1 Paul says, "...knowledge puffs up, but love builds up." The foundational instinct of apostles is love. When you read the books written by apostles in the NT, you find them laced through with love. Love is the glue that holds the whole Kingdom together. Love is the very motivation of Jesus coming to earth to redeem us. Knowledge cannot substitute for this love. By its nature and its relationship to good and evil, knowledge will puff us up and make us proud. So we have apostles, oriented to love and motivated by love. And we have teachers, oriented to knowledge and motivated by knowledge. One will be subject to the other. The NT teaches that teachers must come under apostolic authority or become apostles themselves.

Paul's order in I Corinthians 12:28 is not just a suggestion. Apostles first. Prophets second. Teachers third. It is apostolic order. Here is why it is so important. Apostles motivate us and cause things to happen in the present. Prophets motivate us and orient us to the future. Teachers motivate us and orient us to the past. The truth is that we need all three. But when prophets are first, there is an unhealthy absorption with the future. And very often, the tasks of the present are left undone. When teachers are first, there is an unhealthy absorption with the past. There is great effort expended to apprehend the miracles of the past, but none to find them in the present. But when apostles are first, the future and the past flow into the present and actually find their purpose in the present. The futuristic ministry of the prophets is harnessed to bring forth fruit in this world we live in the present. The historical nature of the teachers' ministry is incorporated as vital knowledge to enhance the present Kingdom advance. Obviously, this is the ideal. The church has fallen short of Paul's apostolic order many times. But this is a new day! The giftings can work together in our world as they did in the book of Acts.

Chapter Six- Who's in Charge in Church History?

There is a profound tragedy in the early history of the Christian church. This tragedy is the repetition of the mistake of ancient Israel. After the loss of kings and prophets, the teachers ruled. They ruled in the absence of kingly and prophetic oversight from within the people of God. Without this corrective oversight, the teachers were puffed up by the knowledge they had acquired through great efforts and great learning institutions. The tragedy deepens when you understand that the Church, having this example in front of them, repeated the same mistake. In the process the powerful church of the book of Acts became the powerless church of the Church Fathers.

The first step in the process of decline was the rise of the bishops. What the apostles were to the first century church, the bishops became to the second and third century church. It is not that there should be no bishops. The NT clearly teaches their office and role. The problem is that the leadership of the church began to slip away, out of the hands of the apostles and more and more into the hands of the bishops. As we enter the second and third centuries, the bishops are almost always teachers, not apostles. Therefore, their ministry orientation is to lead by knowledge and its dissemination. Their claim to authority was that someone with a relationship to apostolic authority laid hands on them. Whether they themselves moved in that authority was negotiable. Over time, the popular persuasion arose that those with the most knowledge must be the best leaders. Sounds kind of like the Greeks, doesn't it?

As teachers came more and more into the driver's seat, prophetic ministry was devalued. The greatest prophecies and the greatest miracles were those that happened a long time ago. The prophecies and miracles of the present did not seem as authentic, and their value was allowed to slip. There has always been a tension between prophets and teachers in the community of the people of God. Prophets are always leading out by revelation. Visions, dreams, oracles, are the currency the prophets love to spend. Teachers are always leading out by information. Their currency is charts, diagrams, studies, research, and philosophical reflection. Teachers spend these freely on their students. Unless there is an authority higher than either of these two, they will continue to oppose each other. But that authority has been placed in the apostles. In fact, when the prophetic and the didactic meet and kiss, the apostolic springs forth.

Another reality of the decline in the church was the decreasing frequency of healings and miracles. In the second century, the works of Polycarp and Justin Martyr tell us of prophecies, healings, and deliverances from demons. Revelatory and miraculous ministry was available in the second century. Bishops in general were men whose knowledge came from the lived experience of Christian life in a hostile environment. But as time went by, bishops were more and more men of rational knowledge, great teachers, but with little or no practical lived experience of prophetic and apostolic authority. To them, apostles were great persons of the past. Prophets in the present were trouble. So the stage was set for a repeat of Israel's great decline.

The best-known prophetic movement of the Early Church was the Montanists. They were known for their emphasis on ecstatic prophecy, healings, and miracles. They certainly did not do everything right, as we read in the historical record. But their desire to see the power of God in their times is commendable. And they certainly do not deserve the title of heretics. This was placed on them in later times, mostly by "Sadducees" who did not believe in revelatory miracles. The bishops, who should have provided apostolic oversight, with corrections, did not. So most of what we hear about from the era of the Montanists is the excesses. I believe, without endorsing every one of their practices, that they were a revival movement, sent by God to restore to the Church the supernatural power that had already been lost.

Tertullian, considered one of the fathers of the Early Church, embraced Montanism in the early third century. He admired their ability to follow the leading of the Holy Spirit, and the spontaneous nature of their worship. Tertullian himself made a powerful statement about the church and the intellectual world.

> Whence spring those "fables and endless genealogies," and "unprofitable questions," and "words that spread like a cancer?" From all these, when the apostle would restrain us, he expressly names philosophy as that which he would have us be on our guard against. Writing to the Colossians, he says, "See that no one beguile you through philosophy and vain deceit, after the tradition of men, and contrary to the wisdom of the Holy Ghost." He had been at Athens, and had in his interviews (with its philosophers) become acquainted with that human wisdom which pretends to know the truth, whilst it only corrupts it, and is itself divided into its own manifold heresies, by the variety of its mutually repugnant sects. **What indeed has Athens to do with Jerusalem? What concord is there between the academy and the Church? What between heretics and Christians?**...Away with all attempts to produce a mottled Christianity of Stoic, Platonic, and dialectic composition! We want no curious disputation after possessing

Christ Jesus, no inquisition after enjoying the gospel! With our faith, we desire no further belief.[1]

With this statement, Tertullian condemns the mingling of Greek philosophy with Christian doctrine. This is the activity of Marcion, who taught that Jesus only appeared to be human, because pure spirit cannot contaminate itself with matter (Plato). But in raising these questions, Tertullian gives us a valuable gift. Athens and Jerusalem are incompatible. The academy, controlled by teachers of Greek philosophy, is incompatible with the Church, founded on the apostles and prophets. There are indeed two kinds of wisdom here, one proceeding from the tree of the knowledge of good and evil, and the other proceeding from the tree of life. It is teachers, apart from apostolic oversight, who mix these waters, and over time, the product is a powerless church.

There was a subtle transformation taking place in the days of Tertullian. It began even before his time. I believe without realizing it, he contributed to the elevation of the practice of refuting heretics. When you elevate that practice to the highest place, the greatest honor belongs to those who can do it best. And in the

---

T.H.Bindley, trans. *On the Testimony of the Soul and On the 'Prescription' of Heretics* (SPCK) London-New York: 1914 Chapter 7.

third, fourth, and fifth centuries teachers refuted heretics tirelessly, and became famous in the process. Refutation of heretics became the highest value. Those who could do it best became the leaders, and guess what? They were almost exclusively teachers who had no apostolic authority over them. Oh, if you had asked them, they would have told you they did, because they were obedient to the bishop. But as far as signs and wonders, healings and miracles attesting to a Gospel that had the power to change lives, little was expected, and little was produced. The focus was changed to the preservation of the existing order. After all, the days of the great miracles and healings were in the past, right?

I have good reasons to believe in the veracity of present-day prophecy. One day I entered a room in the village of Nandikotkur, South India. An 88-year-old pastor named Nagi came up to me and began hugging and kissing me. This is not a typical Indian greeting. I had never seen this man, but he seemed to know me. I responded as best I could, and finished the time of interaction with the pastors who were supporting our meeting in the city. Our invitation to Nandikotkur happened four months earlier. We were staying in a hotel in the city, while ministering at a nearby town. The Hindu manager of the hotel heard about what we were doing, and asked for a private meeting. This man was a "Cornelius" in his city, a seeker for truth. He had heard about our meeting in the other town. With tears in his eyes, he begged us to come to do a crusade in Nandikotkur. After listening to him for awhile, I told him we would come in one year. This was in December of 2002. He was satisfied with this answer.

I went back home to the USA, and was going about my business in traveling preaching ministry. In late January, I received a call canceling a conference I was to speak at in a western state. I was surprised by this, and immediately went to prayer. The opening in my schedule now was in mid-March. I cried out to God, asking Him where I should go now that the conference was cancelled. After a long time of prayer, I was hearing nothing. But a still, small voice was speaking, so quiet; I couldn't hear it at first. The voice was saying, "Nandikotkur, Nandikotkur." When I first recognized this name, spoken to me by God, I said, "Oh, Nandikotkur, I'm going there in December." But the voice grew louder until I realized God was telling me to go in March instead of December! Our March trip to India was all set, I thought. We'll have our pastor's conference in the city of Hyderabad, and then our crusade in Sangareddi. But now the week immediately following was open as well. I called my contacts in India to ask if a crusade could be prepared in five weeks. They said, "No problem, sir, just send large money!" I called the pastors who were going with me to ask if they could stay in India an extra week. All three said, "Yes, no problem." Last I called our travel agent to change our tickets. He said, "I'm glad you called at 4:00pm today, because after 4:30, I would have had to charge you $1000 to make these changes." It pays to listen to the voice of God and obey. So we arrived in March instead of December.

After my encounter with Nagi, I wondered why he had greeted me that way. It was very unusual. Our night meetings on the grounds were going very well, first with hundreds, and then thousands being saved. Many were being healed and delivered from evil spirits. After the first four days of meetings, I was invited to speak at Nagi's church on Sunday morning. I said to myself, "Now I will get some answers as to why he hugged and kissed me a few days earlier. We had a wonderful service, followed by a meal. As we were eating, I was seated next to Nagi. He said to me, "I suppose you were wondering why I hugged and kissed you when you came into the city." I said, "Please tell me!" Nagi said, "Fifteen years ago, I received a burden for your nation, the USA. I began praying hours each week for your country. After four months of this, I had a vision, and with it there came a word of prophecy for Nandikotkur." God said, "A man is going to come here from the USA, and preach in this village, and thousands will repent of their sins. There will a major impact on the city. The clinic will be empty of sick people because they will be healed at the meetings." Nagi waited on God, and then he delivered the prophecy to several small Christian gatherings in the city. The Christians said, "Nagi, we greatly respect you as a Christian leader in this city, but we cannot accept this prophecy. Those American preachers don't come to towns like this; they stay in the big cities." After this rejection of his prophecy, Nagi did not get bitter, he got better. He gathered a band of intercessors around him, and *for fifteen years they prayed* for the fulfillment of this prophecy. Next, Nagi said to me, "When I saw you in the room several days ago, I said to myself, 'That's the man I saw in the vision fifteen years ago! He's here in the village now!'" When I heard this, I was filled with joy. I was amazed at the power of God to predict in advance that I would be there fifteen years ahead of time!

As we drove through the streets of Nandikotkur that night for the last meeting in the crusade, the streets of the city were nearly empty. This was unusual, because this is the time when everyone comes out into the cool night air in winter in South India. I turned to Pastor Stephen, who was guiding us, and said, "Stephen, where are all the people?" He said, "Sir, I believe they're out at the meeting." And so they were, thousands and thousands of people, seeking Jesus! There was a powerful tangible anointing that night. I prophesied over the town, that it would become a regional center for the power of God to be displayed. There were government leaders present. I prophesied over each one of them. And guess who stood on the platform at the end of the service, completely delivered from the alcoholism that bound him? The Hindu hotel manager who had invited us in the first place. Thank you, Jesus!

Nagi was there, too, weeping as he saw with his own eyes the fulfillment of what he had seen and heard in the spirit fifteen years earlier. I am really glad that I went to Nandikotkur in March instead of December in 2003. In August of that same year, I received an e-mail from Nagi's grand-daughter, telling me that he had passed away. I'm sure if we had gone in December, many wonderful things would have happened and many souls would have been saved, but Nagi would not have seen with his own eyes the fulfillment he labored and fought for. But he did see them, and I am greatly anticipating seeing him in heaven!

So I conclude that prophecy is for today. The ministry of the prophet is worth contending for. Standing alongside teachers, prophets can speak the word of the Lord in a way others cannot. One of the first signs of decline in the church is the loss of prophecy, healings, and miracles. We do not have to live in the backwash of the mistakes of the early church fathers. For centuries, the church has depended on words spoken by teachers, isolated from prophets and apostles. But God is showing up in power and authority once again. The powerless church of Church History is becoming the powerful church of the end of this age!

Chapter Seven- Apostolic Ministry in the Present

In this chapter, I want to lay out the means by which you can identify, and enter into, apostolic ministry. The big lie that has prevailed for centuries is that apostles are a small, elite group. Cessationists have confined them to only the twelve in the Gospels and the book of Acts. And even those who believe in the present activity of apostles many times restrict this office in a most unbiblical way.

In the Bible, more people than the twelve were called apostles, and two of them were women (Romans 16:7)! Apostle Paul is the obvious example, and there are others. The apostolic office was larger than the twelve, even in the first generation of Christians. Should we expect less today? We need thousands of apostles, not a few.

It is the design of heaven that apostles lead us into the battle against hell. When the teachers are in charge, we don't even know we are in a war. Jesus' commands were simple, not complex. Heal the sick; cleanse the lepers, cast out demons. When apostles are in charge, we wage war against the kingdom of darkness. Demons are exposed and cast out, sometimes when we are not expecting it!

A number of years ago, I was conducting a crusade in a village in India called Banaganapalle. Hundreds were coming to Jesus in repentance each night, and many people were being healed. On one of the nights, after the altar call and salvation prayer, I gave a second call for healing of sicknesses. More than two thousand people massed to the front to receive prayer. Understanding there was no way to lay hands on each of them, I began praying *en masse*, rebuking diseases and infirmities that the Holy Spirit was bringing to my consciousness. An unusually strong manifestation of the presence of God came into that place. As I continued doing this for several minutes, a woman was thrown to the ground by a demon spirit. As I watched, still rebuking diseases and illnesses, she got to her hands and knees. Her face was the hideous mask of a demon spirit. I kept on with my commanding prayer, and the presence of Jesus came stronger. The woman got to her feet, struggling and fighting all the way up. Her face was changing, and it became radiant, as the evil spirit left her. I could read her lips. She was saying, "Hallelujah!" a word she had just learned that night. Ten minutes later we had her on the platform, testifying. She told how she had been controlled by the evil spirit for seven years. She was married to a husband, and could bear him no children. Oftentimes she would wander off into the forests for days. Her family would have to search for her to bring her back. But now, she was set free! While she was giving the testimony, the Holy Spirit spoke to me, "When she's finished, lay your hand on her, I want to fill her now!" I laid my hand on Krishna's head, and a tangible fire I could feel with the senses of my skin went down my arm and into her. She began speaking in tongues, and became so heavy with the presence of God that three men were needed to hold her up! She was lost in the presence of Jesus for well over an hour.

Later, as I traveled in that general part of India, I would hear things about Krishna. One day in a village sixty kilometers away, I encountered Pastor Jeremy from Banaganapalle. He told me how his church had tripled in size after the crusade. But he was intent on telling me about Krishna. He said that she was the leading evangelist of his church. She was constantly in the marketplace, winning people to Jesus. I somehow knew I would see Krishna again.

Three and a half years after the first time, we returned to Banaganapalle to do a crusade again. When we arrived in the city, I asked for Krishna to be brought to me. We exchanged greetings, and I found she was happily serving Jesus, as had been reported to me. I asked her if she would share her testimony of what happened to her in the meeting three and a half years ago. She said that it would be a pleasure for her. Here is a scene that is burned into my memory: Krishna, standing on our platform, telling the crowd of the torment of the evil spirit, and then of her deliverance. She was holding the hand of her two-year son in her left hand and her infant daughter in her right arm!! Thank you, Jesus!! This is the woman whose life was ruined, controlled by an evil spirit. But now she is an evangelist in her village, bearing children to her husband, and glorifying God!!

This is the power of the Gospel! This is the ability of Jesus to take a life that had been ruined, and rebuild it through a power encounter. The apostolic commitment is that Jesus' victory on the cross and in the resurrection gives us absolute authority over the powers of darkness. This simple truth stands at the center of Christianity. Just about everywhere Jesus went, He was casting out demons. The warfare was constant, and Jesus always prevailed. We will prevail, too, when we stand in the simplicity of the Gospel.

Apostolic ministry is not far away, it is very close at hand. The key identifying mark of apostolic ministry is love. Jesus, who was the five-fold ministry in one man, was constantly touching people with this perfect love from the Father. When the apostles are in charge, love is the foundation for everything. When teachers are in charge, knowledge is the basis for everything. This is because of the differences in the giftings, as we have explained above. Knowledge is very important, and so is the ministry of teachers. But knowledge must be subject to love. That is why teachers must be subject to apostles or become apostles themselves. Only then will we come into alignment with the scripture, "Knowledge puffs up, but love builds up" (I Corinthians 8:1).

In Kahama, Tanzania we had started the first night of meetings. We had a wonderful time of worship, followed by a mass healing prayer over the people. The testimonies were flowing like streams after a spring rain. Right in the middle of these wonderful testimonies, a madman burst out from the crowd, running straight at the platform. He collided with the steel undergirding and fell to the ground, flopping around like a fish. Two uniformed policemen and three other men grasped him by the arms and legs and dragged him away to the side. We continued the meeting with preaching and an amazing altar call where hundreds of people gave their lives to Jesus. When I sent the team down to pray for the sick, I followed them and stood down on the ground myself. Two African brothers who looked like football linebackers lifted the madman and carried him to stand in front of me.

This madman was known to the people of the village. He lived in the dumpsters, feeding on garbage and whatever people would throw to him. He was totally deranged, clothed only with a shirt that was tied around his waist by the sleeves. He smelled bad, he looked bad, and his life was a mess. But now when I looked at him up close, *I loved him.* And I began to believe that he could be set free. I can't rationally explain this, but I knew in my heart that God loved him, and I loved him, too. This man had many demons. His case was very similar to the madman of Gadara who Jesus ministered to in Mark chapter 5. I remembered what Jesus did when He was in this situation, and after naming three or four demon spirits by name, I said loudly, "Go!" As I watched, the demons came off of him, out of him, whatever level of ministry was needed, it was there. He did not thrash around or roll on the ground. He just stood there, while I watched dozens, then hundreds of demons flee from him. I believe he was being held by mighty warring angels sent from heaven itself. His eyelids fluttered. His head moved from side to side. But he stood in place. I felt like I had been transported into a Biblical scene. Indeed it was, but it was in the present, up close and personal, and I was involved.

I stepped up and grabbed the madman in my arms and held him to myself for about seven or eight minutes. As far as I know, it was the first time he was held by anyone in a long, long, time. More demons came out of him. People ask, "How can you hold a man to yourself who you know is full of demons?" I respond that *I have God in me.* I am full of the presence of the living God by the Holy Spirit. And He is way more powerful than any demon in Satan's kingdom. The former madman was becoming conscious of himself. I tried helping him with his shirt, the only garment he had, as he tried to get his arms in the sleeves. I remember praying, "Lord, please let it be long enough to cover him!"

We turned the former madman over to two pastors from the village. They took turns sleeping and watched him all night. They were familiar with his history in the village. The next day they called Pastor Eugene, our crusade director, and reported the following: he took a bath, he eats food that is set before him, he carries on a conversation, and he is wearing the clothes we gave him. The pastors said, "As far as we can tell, he is OK!" I said to Eugene, "Tell them to bring him back to the meeting tonight, so he can testify to the crowd. We have video of the former madman, standing clothed, in his right mind, telling the crowd of his deliverance the previous night. We all rejoiced, some wept tears of joy, and the name of Jesus was exalted!

When we returned to the USA from that trip, I called my spiritual father, who lives in another state. After some greetings, he asked me, "What happened on Wednesday morning?" I quickly calculated the difference in time zones. I said, "That was early

Wednesday evening, right when I was standing in front of the madman." He said, "I had a burden of prayer for you that would not release for three hours." Then I understood why it had been easy, not difficult, to bring deliverance to the madman. The battle was being fought in prayer from thousands of miles away, by my own spiritual father. He obviously was listening to the leading of the Holy Spirit. We have had contact and follow-up with the former madman. He has a job, supporting himself, and lives in a house on the north end of the village. He is attending a Spirit-filled church nearby.

I trust that you can see from this story that love is the key to advancing the Kingdom. The Kingdom advance that was needed in Kahama was the deliverance of a man who everyone knew, whose case was impossible. But God hasn't seen impossible yet (Luke 1:37). In the relationship between Pastor Eugene and myself, there is a unity which brings forth the apostolic ministry. We fully expect, every time we go into a meeting, that we will see signs and wonders as Jesus promised. And they happen all the time. So love must lead, guide, and motivate us in everything we do. Everything the New Testament says about love is true. And it is foundational to an apostolic ministry.

I believe that Father God is raising up fathers to guide a new generation of spiritual leaders. Here the statement of the Apostle Paul to the Corinthians becomes so important: "For though you might have ten thousand instructors in Christ, you do not have many fathers; for in Christ Jesus I have begotten you through the gospel" (I Corinthians 4:15). The relationship between a father and a son or daughter is different than that between a teacher and a student. A father indeed teaches and instructs, but in a very different way than a teacher. A father has a personal stake in the success of the son or daughter. A father's greatest success occurs when his son or daughter succeeds. How different this is from the knowledge-based leadership we are all so familiar with. In this emerging paradigm, which is nothing more or less than reclaiming the power and authority of the New Testament church, the relational bonds of love become the true and authentic platform of God's power.

Chapter Eight- Receiving Apostles in a Celebrity Culture

In our Western world most of us live in a celebrity culture. We are constantly bombarded with news and information about celebrities. Stories about movie stars and politicians take the lion's share of most newscasts. You would think that what really matters is the details of these lives. The unconscious persuasion exists that if you are rich and famous and on TV, your life really matters. The church is not immune from this influence. And I understand that there are valid ministries which use TV as a medium of expression of the Gospel. But all this attention to celebrities has had an effect on us. There is something about the word apostle in Christian circles that makes us think-celebrity. If you study the lives of the apostles in the book of Acts, you will find that they were anything but celebrities. Apostle Paul says in I Corinthians 4:9, "For I think that God has displayed us, the apostles, last, as men condemned to death; for we have been made a spectacle to the world, both to angels and to men." The Greek word translated spectacle here is <u>theatron,</u> from which we derive our English word theater. In the depravity of the ancient Greek theater, the final scene of the drama always led to the death of the <u>moros,</u> the fool. And they were literally executed on the stage many times. In verses 11-13, Paul says, "To the present hour we both hunger and thirst, and we are poorly clothed, and beaten and homeless. And we labor, working with our own hands. Being reviled, we bless; being persecuted, we endure; being defamed, we entreat. We have been made as the filth of the world, the offscouring of all things until now." This hardly sounds like the life of a celebrity! This sounds like the life of a man on a mission, a man with a heavenly vision to be played out on an earthly forum. And so it is with apostles.

What can we do as the Western church to enhance and advance the ministry of the apostle? First, we can stop treating them like celebrities. We can honor them with the true honor of faith, not the false honor of this present world. We can expect that apostles will be found in many places we did not expect to find them. Many people who are called pastors of local churches are actually apostles. Many who are called missionaries are really apostles. And many who have received the call to be bishops or superintendents in church structures are actually called by God to be apostles. It seems that within denominations and church structures, "apostle" is a term to be avoided. But the ministry of the apostle is a crying need of our day.

I believe that apostles in our present age have a ministry of returning us to primitive Christianity. By this I mean first the vision and practice of ministry by which Jesus ministered, and second, the vision and practice by which the church was established in the book of Acts. I do not mean that to be authentic, Christians must copy particular historical patterns of dress, physical appearance, styles of music, etc. But the timeless values of the supernatural intervention of the hand of God into a human life, these are the primitive patterns toward which the apostles lead us.

We landed in Bangalore, India, and departed quickly on a ten-hour drive over terrible roads. Our five-day crusade started that evening, and I for one, did not want to be late. After several hours of driving as fast as we could on roads that were half pavement and half holes with rocks in the bottom, we stopped in a tiny village for water. A young man was sent to buy some bottles of water for us. As I stood under the open hatch of the vehicle for shade from the burning sun, a small group of people approached. One of them was a young man who had his right hand and forearm wrapped in a gauze bandage. Through the interpreter, I said, "What happened to your arm?" He said, "I broke it fifteen days ago. I cannot move my fingers, and I do not know what will happen to me. There is no clinic in this village, or anywhere nearby." I said to him, "I am here today because I believe in Jesus. He has the power to heal your arm! Would you like me to pray for you?" He said that he would, so I laid my hand on his head, and began to pray with my eyes open. I wanted to watch those fingers of his right hand, because I believed they were going to move. As I watched with my eyes, during the prayer for him, his fingers began to open and close! I said, "What is happening?" He said, "The pain in my arm is becoming less and less, and I can move my fingers!" I said, "This is the power that is in the name of Jesus. He loves you so much that He healed you here today when we prayed for you!" He was now ready, and received Jesus as his savior. Just then, our young man returned with the bottles of water. We had to continue our trip, so I said to the young man who had just been healed, "I have a favor to ask of you." He said, "What is it?" I said, "Would you please tell everyone in this village what Jesus did for you? He said, "I will, sir!" We drove off, rejoicing that primitive Christianity was still available. Living in primitive Christianity does not mean being crude or ill-mannered with people. It means treating them like Jesus did. And like the apostles did in the book of Acts.

Another way we can honor and help apostles is to drop the phony façade of the pseudo-scientific world of the twenty-first century. Primitive Christianity concerns itself with healings, miracles, and casting out demons. When the teachers are in charge, the supernatural world is explained out of existence. The leading Sadducee of the twentieth century was Rudolf Bultmann. Through his teachings and books, he had tremendous influence over the Western church. He believed that demons, angels, and supernatural healings are all part of an archaic worldview. These things cannot possibly coexist in a world that has planes, trains, and automobiles, according to Bultmann. So he launched a massive demythologizing project. The purpose? To make the New Testament understandable to people who live in the modern world. He will explain away these supernatural elements of the New Testament and substitute rational, modern equivalents to the modern mind. Along the way, the power of the gospel to change lives is lost. Christianity becomes another actor on the stage of world religions. All talk and no power. A rhyming jingle came into existence:

> Hark the herald angels sing, Bultmann is the latest thing;
> Or they would, had he not, demythologized the lot!

This is the tragedy of teachers being in charge without apostolic oversight in the modern world. Now the quest for more knowledge and its expression actually changes the content and value of the message. Is the belief in the existence of demons in the way? Teachers can explain it away for you. But somehow you know that Jesus Himself was dealing with real spiritual beings in those NT stories, not figments of an ancient imagination. Do demons really exist in advanced Western cultures?

I was in a town in western Minnesota, nearing the end of a Sunday morning service. I asked those with needs in their lives to come forward to receive prayer at the altar. A young man stood in front of me. He dug into his eyes and pulled out a pair of thick contact lenses, which he handed to me. He said, "I am legally blind. I want to be healed." I put the contact lenses in my pocket and began praying for him. We both felt God's presence, but there were many more people to pray for. I said to him, "Stand here and let this Presence come over you. I will return and pray for you some more." I prayed for many people that morning, and then I returned to the young man. When I laid my hands on him, he jerked and fell to the floor on his back. He arched his back and began crabwalking around in a circle! This is not usually what happens in church on Sunday morning! I had seen this manifestation of the presence of a demon spirit years earlier in Chicago. I held my hand over the chest of the young man and commanded the demon to go in the name of Jesus. In a few seconds, his body collapsed to the floor, no more crabwalking. But as his body hit the floor, he spun over to lie on his belly. Next I heard a loud gasp as he breathed in and was filled with the Holy Spirit. The Presence of the living God was stronger than the presence of the demon spirit. And now he was basking in the peace and joy of the Holy Spirit. We sat and watched him for about a half hour. Finally he sat up and began to speak in

English. His eyes were getting better and better. Here was a clear case of a young man being delivered from the oppression of a demon spirit in the USA! His baptism in the Holy Spirit and healing immediately followed his deliverance.

The reason the primitive church was able to turn the world upside down is that they realized Jesus gave them a second chance at being the Israel of God. Now the prophet, priest, and king had become the apostle, prophet, evangelist, pastor, and teacher. With these ministries and offices in place, the primitive church healed the sick, cast out demons, and raised the dead. The apostles, helped by the prophets, (Ephesians 2:20) were leading the way, further assisted by evangelists, pastors, and teachers. Teachers were never in the number one leadership spot (I Corinthians 12:28) in the NT except once. That was when Israel after the flesh, in the persons of the scribes, Pharisees, and chief priests, teachers all, were opposing Jesus. I believe that what is needed in this hour is recognition of apostles as leaders. For example, people who are called pastors of churches who are constantly reaching for places to plant churches are probably apostles, not pastors. We also need apostolic prophets, apostolic evangelists, apostolic pastors and apostolic teachers. These latter will submit to the leadership of apostles and teach from the heart of God, not from the head of man. In such a condition, the church of the twenty-first century will also turn the world upside down.

The transition we seek is a simple one. No one will be a leader on the basis of knowledge alone. Every leader will be qualified for his/her leadership role by love. Love, not knowledge, will be the supreme value of the church. Under this apostolic mandate the prophets will speak life into the destinies of their hearers. The evangelists will reach out to the lost with the compassion of Jesus. The pastors will comfort and feed the sheep from the Father's heart, and the teachers will flow heavenly truth into earthly ears.

I had a strong reminder of the supremacy of love while ministering in a town in northern Minnesota. In this particular meeting, we had taken the testimony of a young lady who had been healed of terrible abdominal pains. She had undergone four exploratory surgeries with no remedy. Her healing occurred in a nearby town two days earlier *over a cell phone*. There she stood, completely healed by the power that is in the name of Jesus. As I preached that night, I noticed a young man seated on the left side of the building. In spite of the powerful testimony of the healing power of Jesus, he sat with his arms folded and a stony look on his face. At the end of my message, I called the people forward for prayer ministry. After praying for a number of people, I finally got to the young man. He was already receiving prayer from an apostolic pastor, and I joined in. I asked him what he wanted Jesus to do for him and he said, "Nothing. I'm a follower of satan. I enjoy reading the satanic bible." I said, "Why are you here in this church if you are a follower of satan?" He said, "There is a girl in this church who I really like, and I faked getting saved several weeks ago to get her attention." At this point, God took over. I felt a love for this young man that I cannot explain rationally. I said to him, "The God I serve really loves you, and He's going to help you forgive your father for all those terrible things he did to you." He said, "That will never happen!" I said, "We'll see!" And motivated by the love I felt for him, I stepped forward and put my arms around him. Amazingly, I felt his arms press against my back, and I knew something was happening. After a couple of minutes of letting the Father's love soak into him, I led him in a prayer forgiving his human father. I knew this was the key to his situation because of what I had seen in the Spirit earlier when I looked at him. Next I led him in the sinner's prayer. Now there was no more faking, he was getting right with God. When I let go of him, he was shaky. We put a chair under him and he sat down. He said, "I never felt this in the satan meetings." We said, "This is the presence of Jesus and the Holy Spirit!" He was taken home by the pastor, and he shook under the power of God all the way home, a thirty minute drive. Five years later, my wife and I were returning to that church in northern Minnesota. I said to myself, "I really want to see that young man who was a satanist." I called the pastor and asked about him. The pastor said, "He has moved out of the area, and I have lost contact with him." On the second night of the meetings, I was standing in the back of the church and in walked the young man, who had just moved back from a distant city. Five years had gone by, and here he was, loving and serving Jesus! He testified to the crowd that night, and we all rejoiced over the keeping power of Jesus!

Chapter 9- What Are the Apostles in Charge of?

In the previous chapters I have labored to establish a simple, yet profound truth. Apostles and prophets are the foundation of the NT church. Teachers are very important also, but the order given by the apostle Paul in I Corinthians 12:28 is first apostles, second prophets, third teachers. When this order is established, the church is powerful, expansive, and above all, loving. When this order is changed, the church is knowledge-based, exclusive, and turned in on itself. This is especially true when the teachers are in charge. But the question remains- if, by the grace of God, the apostles come to be in charge again, what will they be in charge of?

The first and best answer to this question is that they are in charge of the advance of the Kingdom into the world. Jesus taught us to pray, "Our Father who art in Heaven, Your Kingdom come, your will be done on earth as it is in heaven." (Matthew 6:9, 10) The incredible power of this prayer is that it encompasses the full range of the purposes of God on earth. If the conditions which prevail in heaven could prevail on earth, God's will would be established and done.

The Garden of Eden was a manifestation of this reality. It was a place of perfect beauty and perfection, like heaven. But it was on earth. Adam and Eve were charged with stewardship and were given dominion over this realm (Genesis 1:26-28). For a time, these conditions of heaven on earth prevailed in Eden. But there was another being there. His name is satan. Taking the form of a serpent, he tempted Adam and Eve to partake of the tree of the knowledge of good and evil. The only prohibition God had given them was to not eat of this tree. The tree of life was in the garden, too, and they were not forbidden to eat from it. Satan's goal was to acquire the dominion that was the possession of Adam and Eve. If he could deceive them into disobeying the command of God, he believed this dominion would be his, and he was right about that. In their sin against the love of the Father, Adam and Eve traded away the dominion over the place where heaven ruled on earth. In exchange, they received the mixed knowledge of good and evil. From that point on, it was impossible for humans to receive pure knowledge alone. The knowledge of good, in the natural realm, would always be tainted by the knowledge of evil. Adam and Eve assured this by their personal participation in sin.

With the dominion over the realm of the earth in hand, satan began his evil jurisdiction. Ruling with his fallen angels as principalities, and the demons as the foot soldiers, the earth, and the human race were now their playground. God had already promised the coming deliverer. His coming crushes the head of the serpent while he himself has his heel bruised (Genesis 3:16). Throughout the pages of the Old Testament, we read the tragic story of human beings under wars, pestilences, diseases, famines. All these are the fruit of satan's reign over the realm of the earth. Into this hopelessness and despair, God kept sending revelation. First Abraham, then Moses, then David, and many others received God's truth in the hostile environment of satan's kingdom. Through the OT prophets a powerful truth was expressed in generation after generation. God's kingdom is greater than satan's, and it is coming. When God's kingdom comes, it will be ruled by His king, the Messiah, who will defeat satan's schemes and his rule. A new day of victory and peace will fill the earth. This is the powerful message of Isaiah, Jeremiah, Daniel, Ezekiel, and many others. The prophets, priests, and kings of the OT did not see a difference between the reign of satan, and the realm of satan. Likewise, the OT saints did not see a difference between the reign of God and the realm of God. The Hebrew word they used, <u>mamlakah</u>, carried both meanings. And everyone knew that when Messiah came, He would establish the Kingdom of God.

And so Jesus came. The Son of God in human flesh, He was manifested to destroy the works of the devil. When he announced His message and mission in Matthew 4:17, He said, "The Kingdom of heaven is at hand!" The Greek word used to report this to us is

<u>basileia</u>. Translated "kingdom," this word carries the same two-fold meaning as its OT counterpart. It can mean "reign," that is, the *authority* by which kingly purposes are expressed. But it can also mean "realm," that is, the *place* where the kingly authority is exercised. It is of utmost importance that you grasp this difference in the two meanings of this word.

Think of the difference between ancient Greece and ancient Rome. After the conquests of Alexander the Great, the Greeks ruled the known world. They had the realm of the earth, and they brought their reign to it. Greek language, culture, art, the influence was everywhere. This latter reality is the reign of the Greeks. And in their case, it lasted much longer than their realm. Alexander always left behind Greek soldiers to occupy the lands he conquered. So not only was the land (the realm) conquered, the reign of the Greeks (language and culture) was extended. So when the Greeks were conquered militarily by the Romans, they lost the realm. But their reign, by their language and culture was never defeated by the Romans. In fact, although the Romans had a perfectly good language of their own, Latin, it was Greek that was spoken all over the Roman world for centuries. The Romans also adopted the Greek gods and goddesses, renaming them for use in their world. Hermes became Mercury. Zeus became Jupiter. Poseidon became Neptune, and so on. This example can help you see that reign and realm are two different things. They can, and have, existed apart from each other many times. So when the Greek word <u>basileia</u> is used in the NT, we translate it "kingdom." And we need to ask every time, is it speaking of the *realm* or the *reign*?

Since satan usurped the dominion to himself, there is a constant battle to get it back. Satan does not willingly give up the prize he won through his deception of Adam and Eve. Jesus initiated this battle at a whole new level. He defeated satan at every turn. Then He gave satan the ultimate defeat by dying on the Cross and rising from the dead. We now are the enforcers of Jesus' victory. Satan can be forced to give up the souls, the lives, the health of bodies, if we come in the name of Jesus. But usually, there is a battle.

We were in a village in Rwanda named Kayonza. The appointed time for starting the crusade was 4pm. Our rented van rolled onto the field right on time. As we opened the doors and put our feet on the grass of the field, it began to rain. This is the worst thing that can happen, because the people just begin to leave. The local coordinator, Pastor Celestine, came to me quickly and said, "You Americans can get back in the van and stay dry. We'll try to figure out what to do." There was a beautiful first-night crowd there, and they were beginning to leave because of the rain. I replied to Pastor Celestine, "Sir, with all due respect, we're not going to get back in the van. We're going to stay out here with you and fight against this rain!" He agreed as about 200 Christians gathered under a tent structure on the grounds. We took turns leading in prayer. We prayed in English, in Kenya-Rwandan, and in tongues. After an hour of this warfare prayer, the rain stopped! There were almost no people left on the grounds besides the Christians under the tent. I said, "Let's get the meeting started!" And we sent the worship team up to begin. Some people were healed that night, and after awhile, I got up to preach. I had the smallest altar call I've ever had in a foreign crusade. One ten-year-old boy came up to get saved. I was really glad to see him! I treated him like the next John Wesley. He got truly born again! As we returned to the place we were staying, we suspected that the weather event of the rain was not meteorology.

The second night we arrived at the field at 4pm again. And once again, as we opened the doors of the van and put our feet on the grass of the field, it began to rain. Again the crowd began to melt away like sugar under the rain. So we began to pray. This time we prayed for half an hour, and the rain stopped. Once again, we sent the worship team to their positions. And again I preached to a slightly larger crowd than the first night. More people got healed, and about a dozen responded to repent and believe in Jesus. But you could feel the tension of the spiritual battle in the air. The team and I spent the majority of the third day in prayer. We knew we were in a battle with the kingdom of hell for the lives and souls of many people. We had entered a realm in the nation of Rwanda which was held by satan, and he was enforcing that hold with the authority of his realm. But as we came to the battle with the greater authority in the name of Jesus, we began to smell the fragrance of victory, so to speak.

The third night we pulled our van onto the field at 4pm. By now, we were a little edgy about putting our feet out there, but we did, anyway. I stepped out and looked up, and *it didn't rain*! It wanted to. The clouds swirled from one side to the other. The wind blew from the east, then from the west, and finally from the north. The clouds were black and threatening, but *it could not rain*! I said to Pastor Celestine, "Let's get started!" We started on time, finally. There was powerful worship and praise of the living God. A number of people were healed, even before the preaching. Then I got up to preach. One of our team members went down among the crowd. I am so glad he did, because halfway through my message, he saw a man come out of a small house and walk down the straight street of the village right to the back of our platform. I never saw him, because I was facing the people, preaching the word. This man behind me had a long piece of wood called a rain stick. He was pounding it on the ground, trying to make it rain! He was the local witch doctor. The power of satan's reign even when he had the realm, as well, could not prevail against the authority of the crucified and risen Christ! Finally, in utter disgust, the witch doctor ambled back to his house. That night we broke through! Dozens of people streamed forward to repent and call on the name of Jesus. A woman was healed of two grapefruit-sized tumors on her body. They melted away to nothing under the name of Jesus! The kingdom of hell was forced to back up, and the kingdom of heaven advanced. On the final two nights, hundreds of people repented, many were healed, and received miracles. In this conflict of kingdoms, satan lost, and Jesus won, but there was a battle.

Jesus in the flesh was Messiah, Lord, King, everything we read of Him in the NT. But He came into the world that was the realm of satan. That is why satan could offer it to Jesus as part of His temptation in the wilderness (Matthew 4:8-10). But even though satan owned the realm of earth, and reigned it with his evil realities of sin and death, Jesus could not be bought. Where the first Adam failed, the second Adam succeeded. But He did so in a very unusual way, the way that could not be contained in or produced by a mind under the influence of the knowledge of good and evil.

Jesus' mission was to overturn the reign of satan, and ultimately his realm, as well. He was to do this with no realm of his own on earth. Only the words and power given to Him by Father in heaven would be used in this battle. So when you read the Gospels, this is what you see. Jesus is constantly expressing the Kingdom of Heaven. The sick are healed. The demonized are delivered. The sinful are forgiven. The Kingdom has come. It is the *reign of heaven* extended and manifested here on earth. But it has come without the *realm* of heaven. Jesus made this clear when he stood before Pilate during His trial. In John 18:36 Jesus said, "My kingdom is not of this world. If my kingdom were of this world, my servants would fight, so that I should not be delivered to the Jews. But now, my kingdom is not from here." From these words of Jesus, we understand that while He brought all the glory of His kingdom *reign* in His First Coming, the *realm* is reserved for the Age to Come. Jesus refused to enter the realm of politics and have military action taken on His behalf. In the Garden of Gethsemane, Peter took the sword and cut of f the ear of one of the high priest's servants. Jesus healed the ear, and put it back on, while He was being arrested

Another way of speaking of the Kingdom of God, or the Kingdom of Heaven, is to say it is both present and future. It is already, but not yet. This is the greatness of Jesus' coming to the earth as a man.

He split the ages into two. We live in this present evil age because the *realm* still belongs to satan. But satan's *reign* has been broken. Prophetically, satan is cast down. And practically, satan's kingdom is reduced every time a soul comes to Jesus for mercy, every time a sick body is healed. But this present age is not the age to come. The powers of the age to come have broken into this present evil age (Hebrews 6:5), but the age to come is still future.

So the apostles are in charge of the advance of the Kingdom. The reign of God is expanding constantly as the lives of people are changed from darkness to light, from the power of satan to the power of God. But the question remains: will the *realm* of the Kingdom come in this present age? I believe the answer is no, because Jesus Himself refused to rule by the realm even though He was Messiah, Lord, and King. In His resurrection body, Jesus was asked this question by the apostles. In Acts 1:6, they say to Jesus, "Will you at this time restore the kingdom (realm) to Israel?" Jesus answers by promising the power of the Holy Spirit, by which His followers will become witnesses to Him in all the world (Acts 1:8). In other words, the question about the realm is deferred to the present activity of the disciples under the might and power of the Spirit *in this present age*. The plan of this salvation history is spelled out clearly in Acts 3:19-21. Here the apostle Peter says that in this present age, the proper course of action is to repent and enjoy the refreshing times coming from heaven. Then Jesus will be sent (second coming), but He must stay in heaven *until the times of restoration of **all things***. The coming of the *realm* of God follows, and does not precede, the second coming of Jesus.

In the last several decades, there has been a great increase of the activities of apostles in the earth. Along with this has come the powerful reign of Jesus over the lives of men, women, and children all over the earth. This upsurge has brought with it a great interest in the scope of the authority of apostles on the earth. Some have taught that apostles will be in charge of the *realm* of the kingdom in this present age. The sphere of human life on the planet has been divided into seven areas, with the understanding that Christians, under the leadership of the apostles, will take over these seven mountains in this age. The problem with this view is that it is not supported by the statements of Jesus and the rest of the NT. When Jesus gave the Great Commission, He commanded us to take the Gospel to the entire world, that is, the people, and the nations. We are to disciple them, baptize them, and teach them to observe Jesus' commandments (Matthew 28:18-20). The territory that is to be conquered is human hearts and minds with salvation and human bodies with healing. The *reign* of Jesus is to be extended all over the earth (Matthew 24:14), and then the end will come. This coming of the end will include the arrival of the *realm* of God to the earth. It will include the second coming of Jesus Himself, who will appear in the clouds, and then come to earth to establish the realm of the Kingdom.

If you have been a Christian very long, you know that not everyone agrees with the statements I have just made about the present and future of the Kingdom. So let me list out the viewpoints which have emerged over the centuries, so that you can make an informed decision about what you believe. There are four viewpoints on these matters which differ from one another. The *dispensational premillenialists* hold a position in which neither the reign or realm of the kingdom are present now. They believe that Jesus came and offered the kingdom to the Jews, who rejected it. So Jesus took it back to heaven when he ascended. The Gospel in this present age is simply preached as truth, with no reign or realm of the Kingdom. The *amillenialists* hold a position in which both the reign and the realm are here now. They do this by spiritualizing the thousand year reign (Revelation chapters 19, 20) into the present age. For them, there is no future millennium because we are living in it now. The *postmillenialists* hold a position which says that because the reign of the kingdom is here, the church must establish the realm, and give it to Jesus at His Second Coming. So the reign and realm are in this present age, but only at the end. The church must labor to establish the realm over politics, media, and every other area of human life. The *historic premillenialists* hold a position that says the reign of the kingdom is here in this present age, but not the realm. The *reign* of the Kingdom is established every time someone repents, every time a sick person is healed, every time a demon is cast out. But the *realm* will be established by Jesus when He returns in the Second Coming. It is this fourth and last view that I believe best represents the full teaching of the New Testament. I do not believe that Jesus told us to establish the kingdom as a realm here on earth. He most certainly commanded us to establish the *reign* of His Kingdom all over the earth. In fact, the apostle Paul expects that Christians will reign in this way when he says, "For if by one man's offense death reigned through the one, much more those who receive abundance of grace and of the gift of righteousness *will reign in life* through the One, Jesus Christ" (Romans 5:17). And in Romans 14:17 he says, "For the kingdom of God is not eating and drinking, but righteousness and peace and joy in the Holy Spirit."

Conclusion

We started this journey together wondering about apostles and their relationship to teachers. Through the scriptures we have explained the supremacy of apostolic love. Through the experiences I have related you have seen it in practical action. This apostolic love brings the supernatural power of God into every situation. This is the leadership mandate of apostles: love breaks through; love finds a way for the revelatory work of God to prosper. Contrast this with the leadership mandate of teachers, which is knowledge. When knowledge is placed above love, the supernatural mission of the church is thwarted. Knowledge-based leadership cannot help itself from leading us into pride. The examples of Israel and of the Early Church show this conclusively.

I leave you with this: love wins! Knowledge puffs up, but love builds up (I Corinthians 8:1). The teachers must submit to apostolic leadership or become apostles themselves. With apostles leading from the positions of "pastor," bishop, elder, superintendent, the powerless church will become the powerful church once again. The world will see who Jesus really is: savior, healer, deliverer, and lover of their souls.

The crying need of our day is to reach people in love and power. Thus the need for apostles has never been greater. The allure of changing the institutions of human society is very great. The power of God is certainly capable of it. But is this what Jesus told us to do? I believe when large numbers of people are saved and delivered in a local area, that societal change will happen. The revivals in Argentina and Brazil during the last century have taught us that. But this bottom-up effect is quite different from the top-down cause of the postmillennialists. This love of the Father is designed to reach people, not institutions. It is people who need to be saved, healed, delivered, not institutions. The healing and deliverance of the institutions is coming. Jesus will rule this earth with a rod of iron in the Age to Come (Revelation 19, 20). In this present age, could we please keep the main thing the main thing? As they submit to apostolic authority, teachers will make their valued contribution of instruction in righteousness. And the attention of the world will be focused, not on apostles, or prophets, or evangelists, or pastors, or teachers, but on the Lord Jesus Christ. He is the center of it all. Every knee will bow; every tongue will confess that Jesus is Lord, to the glory of God the Father! (Philippians 2:10, 11).

SCRIPTURES FOR APOSTOLIC LOVE

Deuteronomy 6:5, Leviticus 19:18, Luke 10:27
You shall love the LORD your God with all your heart, with all your soul, with all your strength, with all your mind, and your neighbor as yourself.

John 13:35
By this all will know that you are My disciples, **if you have love for one another.**

I Corinthians 13:1-13
Though I speak with the tongues of men and of angels, but have not love, I have become sounding brass or a clanging cymbal. And though I have the gift of prophecy, and understand all mysteries and all knowledge, and though I have all faith, so that I could remove mountains, but have not love, I am nothing. And though I bestow all my goods to feed the poor, and though I give my body to be burned, but have not love, it profits me nothing. Love suffers long and is kind; love does not envy; love does not parade itself, is not puffed up; does not behave rudely, does not seek its own, is not provoked, thinks no evil; does not rejoice in iniquity, but rejoices in the truth; bears all things, believes all things, hopes all things, endures all things. Love never fails. But whether there are prophecies, they will fail; whether there are tongues, they will cease; whether there is knowledge, it will vanish away. For we know in part and we prophesy in

part. But when that which is perfect has come, then that which is in part will be done away. When I was a child, I spoke as a child. I understood as a child, I thought as a child; but when I became a man, I put away childish things. For now we see in a mirror, dimly, but then face to face. Now I know in part, but then I shall know just as I am known. And now abide faith, hope, love, these three; **but the greatest of these is love.**

Ephesians 3:17-19

...that Christ may dwell in your hearts through faith; that you, **being rooted and grounded in love**, may be able to comprehend with all the saints what is the width and length and depth and height—to know the love of Christ which passes knowledge; that you may be filled with all the fullness of God.

I John 4:7-19

Beloved, let us love one another, for love is of God; and everyone who loves is born of God and knows God. He who does not love does not know God, for God is love. In this the love of God was manifested toward us, that God has sent His only begotten Son into the world, that we might live through Him. In this is love, not that we loved God, but that He loved us and sent His Son to be the propitiation for our sins. Beloved, if God so loved us, we also ought to love one another. No one has seen God at any time. If we love one another, God abides in us, and His love has been perfected in us. By this we know that we abide in Him, and He in us, because He has given us of His Spirit. And we have seen and testify that the Father has sent the Son as Savior of the world. Whoever confesses that Jesus is the Son of God, God abides in him, and he in God. And we have known and believed the love that God has for us. God is love, and he who abides in God, and God in him. Love has been perfected among us in this: that we may have boldness in the day of judgment; because as He is, so are we in this world. **There is no fear in love; but perfect love casts out fear**, because fear involves torment. But he who fears has not been made perfect in love. We love Him because He first loved us.